Reach Out

Written by Claire Owen

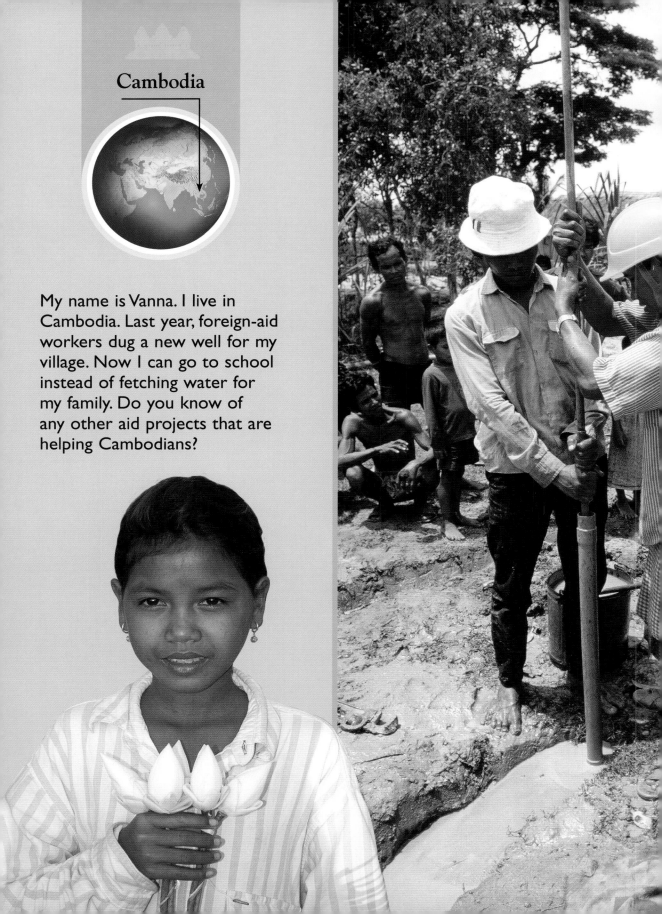

Cambodia

My name is Vanna. I live in Cambodia. Last year, foreign-aid workers dug a new well for my village. Now I can go to school instead of fetching water for my family. Do you know of any other aid projects that are helping Cambodians?

Contents

Wherever you see me, you'll find activities to try and questions to answer.

An Ancient Place

Archaeologists say that people have lived in what is now
called Cambodia for at least 6,000 years. From the first to the
sixth century, the area was known as *Funan*, an important stop
on the sea route between India and China. From the ninth to the
fourteenth century, the Khmer Empire extended over a large part
of Southeast Asia. The Khmer people called their land *Kambuja*
or *Kampuchea*, a name that was westernized as Cambodia.

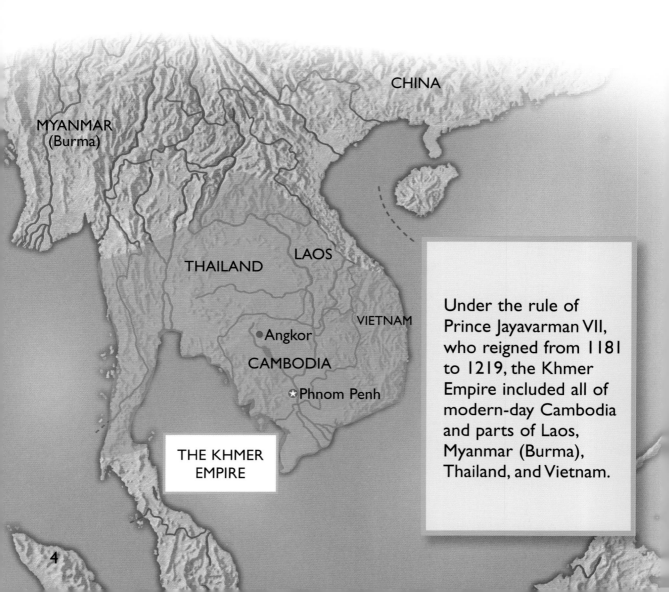

CHINA

MYANMAR
(Burma)

THAILAND

LAOS

VIETNAM

•Angkor

CAMBODIA

☆Phnom Penh

THE KHMER
EMPIRE

Under the rule of
Prince Jayavarman VII,
who reigned from 1181
to 1219, the Khmer
Empire included all of
modern-day Cambodia
and parts of Laos,
Myanmar (Burma),
Thailand, and Vietnam.

Between the years 802 and 1220, the Khmer built more than 100 stone temples at their capital city of Angkor.

For how many years did Jayavarman reign over the Khmer Empire? How many years ago did he come to power?

A frieze from the Bayon temple captures scenes from everyday life in the Khmer Empire. The frieze is more than 1,300 yards long and shows about 11,000 people.

frieze   a strip of carved or painted decoration on a wall

A Growing Empire

During the Khmer Empire, Cambodia was highly productive, and the economy was strong. One reason for the empire's prosperity was the efficient and extensive irrigation system. The Khmer constructed huge artificial lakes called *barays* so that rainfall from the wet monsoon season could be stored and used in the dry season. This meant that two or three rice crops could be grown each year.

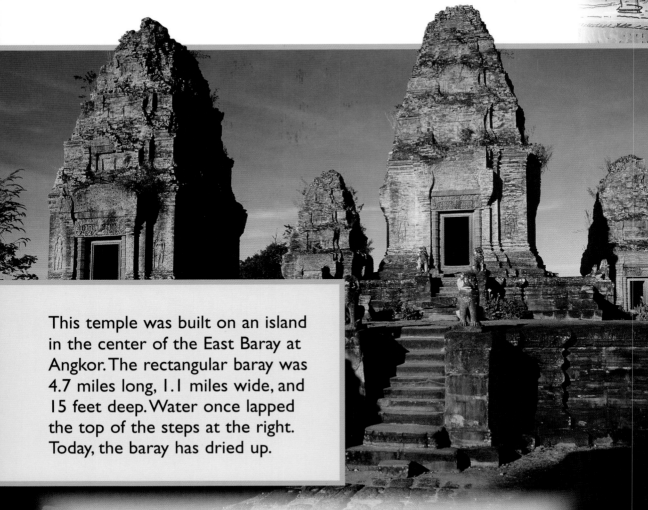

This temple was built on an island in the center of the East Baray at Angkor. The rectangular baray was 4.7 miles long, 1.1 miles wide, and 15 feet deep. Water once lapped the top of the steps at the right. Today, the baray has dried up.

irrigate   to supply with water using ditches or pipes

The West Baray, another huge rectangular reservoir at Angkor, is still used today. The baray covers an area of about 6.25 square miles.

Explain how you would solve the following problems.

1. Which baray at Angkor covered a greater area, the East Baray or the West Baray?

2. For the East Baray, find—

   a. the length, width, and depth of the baray (in yards).

   b. the area covered by the baray (square yards).

   c. the volume (cubic yards).

   d. the number of gallons of water the baray could hold.
   (Hint: One cubic yard holds about 200 gallons.)

3. The length of the West Baray is 3.5 times its width. Which of the following measurements is closest to the width of the West Baray?

   A. 1.3 miles

   B. 1.4 miles

   C. 1.34 miles

   D. 1.35 miles

Troubled Times

By 1432, the Khmer Empire had begun to decline, and the capital was moved to Phnom Penh. Cambodia became part of French Indochina in 1887 and was occupied by the Japanese during World War II. Although the country became independent in 1953, years of conflict and civil war followed. Millions of people died, and much of the country's infrastructure was destroyed. Today, Cambodia receives foreign aid to help its people recover from the ravages of war.

In 1975, a brutal organization known as the Khmer Rouge forced almost all of the people living in Phnom Penh to leave the city and work in the rice fields.

infrastructure   systems and buildings for basic facilities and services, including water, power, transportation, communication, health, and education

Up to one-fourth of Cambodia's population was killed by the Khmer Rouge or died as a result of starvation and overwork in the rice paddies. This tower was erected in memory of the people who died in what became known as the "killing fields."

Since 1979, about 60,000 Cambodians have been injured or killed by land mines left over from the war. Aid projects have been set up to clear land mines and to help rehabilitate the injured.

rehabilitate to restore to normal life by training and therapy

9

Foreign Aid

The Khmer Rouge deliberately destroyed many
of Cambodia's schools and hospitals in the 1970s.
As a result, Cambodia today has poorer standards
of health and education than most Asian countries.
Cambodia receives about half a billion dollars
in foreign aid each year. This is less than some
neighboring countries receive, but on a *per capita*
basis, it is one of the highest rates in south Asia.

Economic Aid		
Country	**Aid in 2002 ($)**	**Population**
Bangladesh	913,000,000	144,319,600
Cambodia	487,000,000	13,607,000
China	1,476,000,000	1,306,313,800
India	1,463,000,000	1,080,264,400
Laos	278,000,000	6,217,100
Myanmar (Burma)	121,000,000	42,909,500
Nepal	365,000,000	27,676,500
Pakistan	2,144,000,000	162,419,900
Thailand	296,000,000	65,444,400
Vietnam	1,277,000,000	83,535,600

per capita   per person

Make a Bar Graph

You will need a calculator, a piece of paper, a copy of the Blackline Master, and colored markers or pencils.

1. Use a calculator to find the amount of aid *per capita* for each of the countries on page 10. Round each answer to the nearest cent.

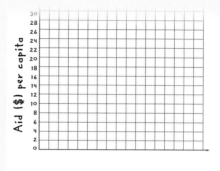

Country	Aid ($) per
Bangladesh	6.33
Cambodia	35.
China	
India	

2. Label the vertical axis. (Choose a scale that will enable you to show all of the *per capita* amounts.)

3. Write the names of the countries along the horizontal axis. (You could show the countries in alphabetical order or in order of the amount of aid they receive *per capita*.)

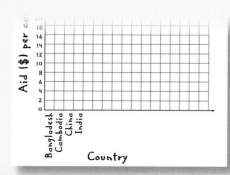

4. For each country, color a bar that shows the *per capita* amount of aid. (Round each amount to the nearest dollar or half dollar.)

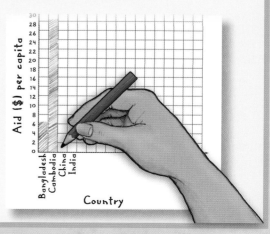

Vital Statistics

Cambodia's infant mortality rate shows that, on average, about 71 babies out of every thousand die before the age of one year. The average life expectancy is about 59 years. These figures are significantly better than for the world's poorest nations, but they are well below the standards of the richest countries.

Rank	Country	Rate
Infant Mortality Rates (Per 1,000 Live Births)		
1	Singapore	2.29
2	Sweden	2.77
3	Hong Kong	2.97
4	Japan	3.26
5	Iceland	3.31
...		
42	United States	6.50
...		
189	Cambodia	71.48
...		
222	Liberia	128.87
223	Mozambique	130.79
224	Sierra Leone	143.64
225	Afghanistan	163.07
226	Angola	191.19

Life Expectancy
(For People Born in 2005)

Rank	Country	Age
1	Andorra	83.51
2	Macau	82.03
3	San Marino	81.62
4	Singapore	81.62
5	Hong Kong	81.39
...		
46	United States	77.71
...		
178	Cambodia	58.87
...		
222	Lesotho	36.68
223	Zimbabwe	36.67
224	Angola	36.61
225	Swaziland	35.65
226	Botswana	33.87

For each of the charts, compare the data for Cambodia with data for the countries that are ranked first and last in the world.

In how many countries is infant mortality higher than in Cambodia? In how many countries is life expectancy shorter than in Cambodia?

Clean Water

One of the most significant factors affecting the health of Cambodian people is access to clean water. Many people rely on the Mekong River for water. As a result of drought and the construction of dams, however, the river is often at a low level. Ground-water sources are drying up, and many village wells have run dry. In short, about 70 percent of Cambodian people do not have easy access to potable water.

In some parts of Cambodia, women or children have to make four or five trips each day to fetch water from rivers or ponds. Providing clean water is a major target of many aid programs.

potable   suitable for drinking

Sinking, or digging, a village well in Cambodia costs between $500 and $1,000.

If every student in your class donated $1 each week, how long would it take to raise enough money to fund a well in Cambodia?

Literacy Matters

During the years of civil war, it was impossible for many Cambodians to attend school. Today, only about three-fifths of Cambodian women and four-fifths of Cambodian men can read and write. This gives Cambodia an overall literacy rate of 69.4 percent, compared to 99 percent in France or Germany and 97 percent in the United States.

In Cambodia, there are about 4,038,500 males and 4,498,600 females 15 years of age and older. Estimate how many of them can read and write.

For each column of figures in the chart below, compare the literacy rate for Cambodia with the highest literacy rate.

Literacy Rates
(Percent of People Age 15 and Over Who Can Read and Write)

Country	Men	Women	Overall
Myanmar (Burma)	89.2	81.4	85.3
Cambodia	80.8	59.3	69.4
Laos	77.4	55.5	66.4
Malaysia	92.0	85.4	88.7
Singapore	96.6	88.6	92.5
Thailand	95.9	90.5	92.6

Young Workers

The median age of people in Cambodia is about 19.5 years. This means that half the population is 19 years old or younger. Cambodia has a much higher proportion of young people than countries such as the United States, where the median age is about 36 years. It is estimated that about half a million Cambodian children were orphaned during the war. Additionally, each year as many as 10,000 children become orphans as a result of AIDS.

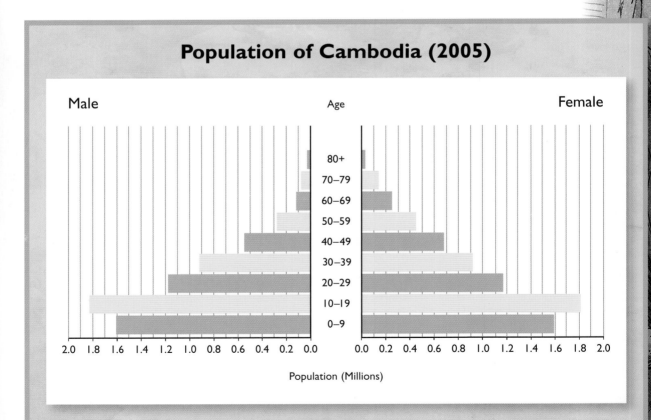

Population of Cambodia (2005)

Male — Age — Female

Population (Millions)

proportion   the relation of one thing to another in size or amount

Many Cambodian children have to work to support themselves or to care for their families.

Figure It Out

Use the graph on page 18 to help answer these questions.

1. Which age group has closest to—

   a. 1,200,000 males?

   b. 900,000 females?

   c. half a million males?

   d. one-fourth of a million females?

   e. 3 million people in all?

For the following questions, round your answers to the nearest tenth of a million.

2. How many Cambodians are—

   a. girls 9 years or younger?

   b. males between the ages of 10 and 19?

   c. between the ages of 30 and 39?

3. Pick an age group on the graph. Estimate—

   a. the number of males.

   b. the number of females.

   c. the total number of people.

A Little Goes a Long Way

One way that people in affluent countries such as the United States can help improve the lives of Cambodian orphans and other children is to sponsor a child. Donating about $20 per month through an aid organization provides a needy child with food, clothing, and an education. The money also helps to fund projects that benefit the child's whole family and community.

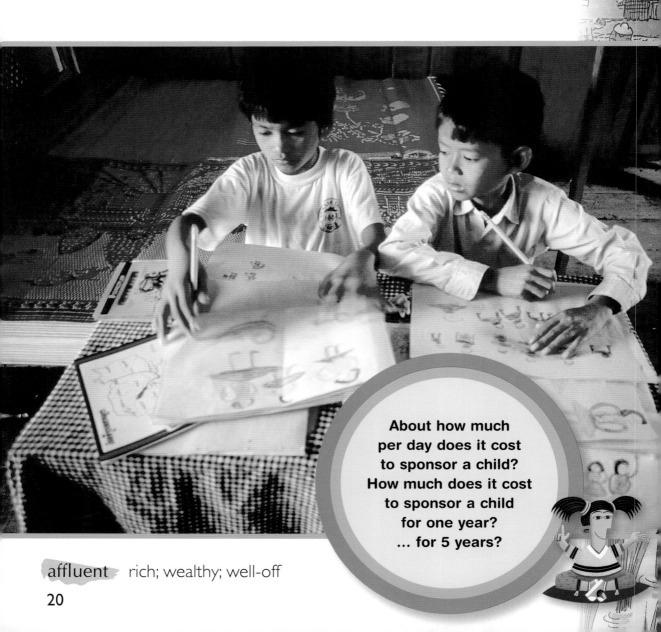

About how much per day does it cost to sponsor a child? How much does it cost to sponsor a child for one year? ... for 5 years?

affluent   rich; wealthy; well-off

Some people find it difficult to buy a gift for friends who "have everything." One Australian aid agency has a clever solution. When you choose gifts from its special catalog, those gifts go to needy people in Asia. Your friends receive a card to show that a gift has been given in their name.

Pretend that you have $80 to spend on gifts from the catalog. What would you buy on behalf of your family or friends?

Gifts that Cost $50 or Less

$5 School Supplies
A year's supply of books, pencils, and paper for one student

$7 Cooking Utensils
A set of household items (including pans, plates, and cups) for a refugee family

$10 Mosquito Net
To reduce the risk of a family contracting malaria, a disease carried by mosquitoes

$20 Kitchen Garden
Seeds and training to help a woman feed her family and earn extra income

$35 Adult Literacy
A short course in literacy and numeracy for an adult who missed out on schooling

$40 Health Care
A year of health-care services for a family, through a community health program

$45 Elementary Education
A year's education for a child in a community-managed school

$50 A Goat
Goats provide milk and meat, and a small herd can be built up in just a few years.

Piggy Banks

Some of the aid donated to Cambodia is for the construction of infrastructure, including roads, bridges, railroads, and telephone networks. Such projects are often very costly but provide benefits for many people. Other projects—such as village banks that "loan" pigs, cows, or rice—help a few people at a time, for a relatively small cost. Both short-term and ongoing projects are helping to build a stronger economy so that Cambodia will eventually become less dependent on foreign aid.

Em Yem received a sow from her village's pig bank. After the sow had nine piglets, Em Yem returned four of them to the bank, gave one to a relative, kept one, and sold the other three.

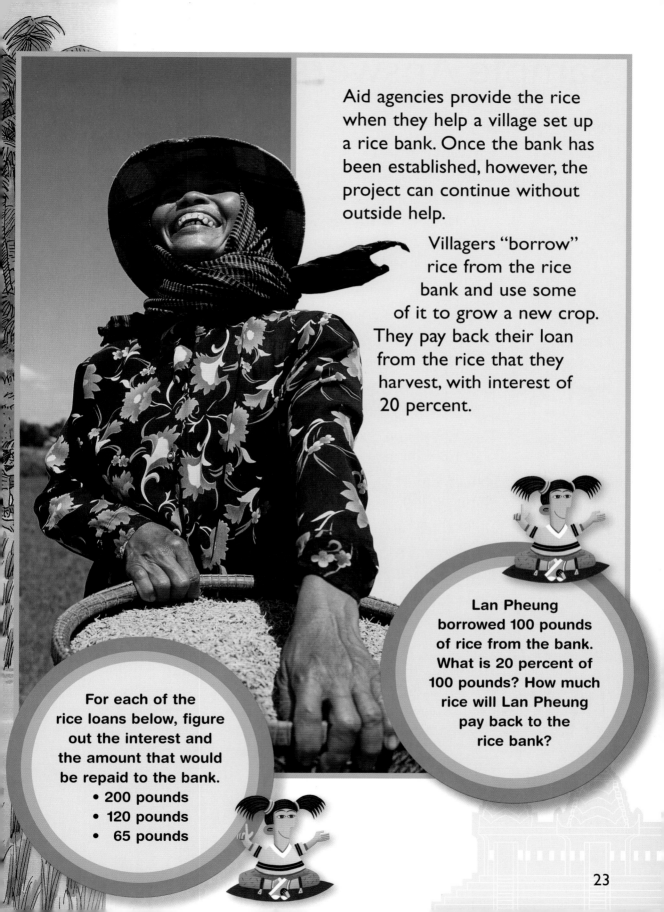

Aid agencies provide the rice when they help a village set up a rice bank. Once the bank has been established, however, the project can continue without outside help.

Villagers "borrow" rice from the rice bank and use some of it to grow a new crop. They pay back their loan from the rice that they harvest, with interest of 20 percent.

Lan Pheung borrowed 100 pounds of rice from the bank. What is 20 percent of 100 pounds? How much rice will Lan Pheung pay back to the rice bank?

For each of the rice loans below, figure out the interest and the amount that would be repaid to the bank.
- 200 pounds
- 120 pounds
- 65 pounds

Sample Answers

Page 5   38 years

Page 7   1. West Baray (Area of East Baray is 5.17 square miles.)

                2. a. 8,272 yards; 1,936 yards; 5 yards
                    b. 16,014,592 square yards
                    c. 80,072,960 cubic yards
                    d. 16,014,592,000 gallons

                3. C

Page 13   37 countries; 48 countries

Page 16   about 3.2 million men and 2.7 million women

Page 19   1. a. 20–29   b. 30–39   c. 40–49
                    d. 60–69   e. 0–9

                2. a. 1.6 million   b. 1.8 million
                    c. 1.8 million

Page 20   about 65 to 67 cents
                $240; $1,200

Page 23   circle at left: 40 pounds, 240 pounds
                24 pounds, 144 pounds
                13 pounds, 78 pounds

                circle at right: 20 pounds, 120 pounds

Use data from page 10 to find the total amount of aid to Cambodia and the three adjoining countries. Use a computer-graphing program to show that information on a pie chart.

Index